Hu

Ryan

*methuen* | drama

LONDON • NEW YORK • OXFORD • NEW DELHI • SYDNEY

METHUEN DRAMA
Bloomsbury Publishing Plc
50 Bedford Square, London, WC1B 3DP, UK
1385 Broadway, New York, NY 10018, USA
29 Earlsfort Terrace, Dublin 2, Ireland

BLOOMSBURY, METHUEN DRAMA and the Methuen
Drama logo are trademarks of Bloomsbury Publishing Plc

First published in Great Britain 2022

Cover design by Guy J Sanders

A catalogue record for this book is available from the British Library.

A catalog record for this book is available from the Library of Congress.

ISBN: PB: 978-1-3503-3957-6
ePDF: 978-1-3503-3958-3
ePub: 978-1-3503-3959-0

Series: Modern Plays

Typeset by Mark Heslington Ltd, Scarborough, North Yorkshire

To find out more about our authors and books visit
www.bloomsbury.com and sign up for our newsletters.

*Human Nurture* was commissioned by Theatre Centre and is a co-production between Theatre Centre and Sheffield Theatres.

**THEATRE CENTRE** **SHEFFIELD THEATRES**

Supported using public funding by

**ARTS COUNCIL ENGLAND**

# THEATRE CENTRE

**Theatre Centre** is a national theatre touring company with a new writing focus, making bold, relatable shows with and for young people in schools, theatres and other settings, including online and in the community. We run Future Makers, a whole new way of supporting young people as artists, creatives, active citizens and leaders. It is central to all of our work and is the key to the way we unlock our young people-centred practice.

Future Makers brings young people, artists, practitioners and teachers together to develop skills, explore big ideas and make work, share skills, explore big ideas. The work is all about amplifying the voice of young people, to develop agency and empowerment, while telling relevant, authentic, and resonant stories. We commission new work from the most exciting contemporary writers and artists in response to themes emerging from Future Makers, and we take this work into schools and theatres across the UK.

During the pandemic in 2020/21 we connected with over 500 schools, with over 55,000 young people watching the film of *Birds and Bees* by **Charlie Josephine**, and hundreds of teachers using our resources to support learning as part of the recovery curriculum.

Founded in 1953, we are an acknowledged leader in our field. Our practice is inclusive and continues to evolve and to be a ground breaking force in developing new writing with and for young people alongside offering vital support and access for networks of drama teachers across the UK. Theatre Centre is predominantly a Learning Organisation working at the grassroots and we have an embedded culture of developing and nurturing everyone involved in or touched by the work.

**www.theatre-centre.co.uk**

# SHEFF!ELD
# THEATRES

**Sheffield Theatres** is home to three theatres: the Crucible, the Sheffield landmark with a world-famous reputation; the Studio, an intimate, versatile space for getting closer to the action; and the gleaming Lyceum, the beautiful proscenium that hosts the best of the UK's touring shows.

Having held the title 'Regional Theatre of the Year' on four separate occasions, Sheffield Theatres is the ticket to big names and local heroes, timeless treasures and new voices. Committed to investing in the creative leaders of the future, Sheffield Theatres' dedicated talent development hub, The Bank, opened in 2019 to support a new cohort of emerging theatre-makers every year.

In November 2021, the Crucible and Studio theatres celebrated their 50th anniversary. The anniversary season includes a theatrical first, with **Chris Bush**'s new trilogy *Rock/Paper/Scissors* to be performed across all three venues with the same cast at the same time, plus the highly-anticipated return of Sheffield-set new musical *Standing at the Sky's Edge*. With music and lyrics by Mercury Prize-nominated **Richard Hawley**, the production won the 2020 South Bank Sky Arts Award for theatre and was named Best Musical Production at the 2019 UK Theatre Awards.

Sheffield Theatres has a reputation for bold new work. Dazzling adaptation *Life of Pi* won four awards at the 2019 UK Theatre Awards, Achievement in Technical Theatre at the Stage Awards and Best New Play at the WhatsOnStage Awards. The show opened in the West End in 2021. This success follows the phenomenal Sheffield musical *Everybody's Talking About Jamie* which started life at the Crucible in 2017, before transferring to the West End, embarking on a UK tour and being turned into a feature film released simultaneously to 244 countries on Amazon Prime in September 2021.

**www.sheffieldtheatres.co.uk**

## CAST

| | |
|---|---|
| Harry | **Lucas Button** |
| Runaku | **Justice Ritchie** |
| Musician | **Neeta Sarl** |

## CREATIVES

| | |
|---|---|
| Writer | **Ryan Calais Cameron** |
| Director | **Rob Watt** |
| | |
| Sound Designer | **Lee Affen** |
| Movement Director | **Yami Löfvenberg** |
| Lighting Designer | **Simisola Majekodunmi** |
| Composer | **Neeta Sarl** |
| Set and Costume Designer | **Tara Usher** |

## PRODUCTION

| | |
|---|---|
| Producer | **Steven Atkinson** |
| Schools Tour Booking and Co-ordination | **Hannah Austin, Niamh Parker-Whitehead** |
| Resource Creator | **Titilola Dawudu** |
| Company Stage Manager | **Elizabeth Bond** |
| Production Manager | **Samantha Nurse** |
| Casting Associate | **Becky Paris** |
| Lighting Programmer | **John Payne** |
| Executive Director | **Emma Rees** |
| Artwork | **Guy J Sanders** |
| Creative Associate | **Monay Thomas** |

## LUCAS BUTTON – Harry

**Theatre credits include:** *The Butterfly Lion* (Chichester Festival Theatre); *Run Sister Run* (Paines Plough/Soho Theatre); *Kes* (Leeds Playhouse); *War Horse* (National Theatre 2017–18 tour); *The Winter's Tale* (English National Opera/Coliseum); *Pinocchio* and *A Tender Thing* (The Dukes); *Alan, We Think You Should Get a Dog* (New Diorama Theatre); *Coram Boy, Ivanov* and *Romeo and Juliet* (RCSSD); *This is Not a Drill* (Tristan Bates Theatre); and *Five, Four, None* (Roundhouse).

**Television credits include:** *Masters of the Air* (Playtone/Amblin); *The Witcher: Blood Origins* (Netflix) and *Worzel Gummidge* (BBC/ Leopard Pictures).

## JUSTICE RITCHIE – Runaku

Justice graduated this year from Guildhall School of Music & Drama.

**Film credits:** Justice recently filmed a small role in the upcoming Paramount film *Dungeons and Dragons*, following which he won the BBC Carleton Hobbs Bursary Award.

## RYAN CALAIS CAMERON – Writer

**Theatre credits include:** *For Black Boys Who Have Considered Suicide When the Hue Gets Too Heavy* (Nouveau Riche/Boundless Theatre/New Diorama Theatre, 2021); *Typical* (Nouveau Riche, Edinburgh Fringe Festival and Soho Theatre Upstairs, 2020) and *Queens of Sheba* (Nouveau Riche, co-written with Jessica Hagan, which won the 2018 Edinburgh Untapped Award; Edinburgh Fringe/ New Diorama Theatre/London and national tour, 2019).

Ryan was the winner of the 2018 Off West End 'Adopt a Playwright Award' for his play *Rhapsody*, which was produced at the Arcola Theatre in March of that year. *Retrograde*, which he wrote on his year of 'adoption', was shortlisted for the 2019 Alfred Fagon Award and Verity Bargate Award 2020.

Ryan is an alumnus of the Royal Court Theatre writers' programme 2017 and the Soho Young Company 2016/17. He is currently under commission to the Royal Court, the Arcola and Soho Theatre, as well as commissions for television.

## ROB WATT – Director

A critically acclaimed director, dramaturg and facilitator, Rob collaborates with writers, young people, communities, poets and designers to make sense of the fractured world we inhabit.

He is currently the Artistic Director for Theatre Centre, regularly teaches at the Royal Central School of Speech and Drama, and is presenter of *The Blurry Bits* podcast with Charlie Josephine. He was previously an Associate for Headlong, headed up the young people's team at the National Theatre, was a Lead Artist at Lyric Hammersmith, an Artist Mentor at the Barbican and Associate Director at Immediate Theatre. He is the chair of SAVVY Theatre's board and governor at Addy and Stanhope School, Lewisham.

**Theatre credits include:** *Birds and Bees* (Theatre Centre); *Acts of Resistance* (Headlong Theatre, Bristol Old Vic, Plymouth Theatre Royal, Brewery Arts Centre, New Perspectives); *Rallying Cry* (Battersea Arts Centre and BBC Contains Strong Words Festival); *Standby for Tape Back-Up* (Summerhall/Soho Theatre/Shoreditch Town Hall/UK tour); *It's Not Too Late to Save the World (and Other Lies)* (Lyric Hammersmith); *Operation Ghost Raven* (The Department & MSC); *The Exorcism* (Battersea Arts Centre); *How to Survive a Post Truth Apocalypse* (Soho Theatre/Roundhouse/UK tour); *Love and Information* (Institute of the Arts Barcelona); *SEXY* (Roundhouse/Bristol Old Vic/UK tour); *Be Prepared* (Underbelly/VAULT Festival); *Party Trap* (Shoreditch Town Hall); *Goosebumps* (The Vaults); and *The Joy of Normal* (Orange Tree Theatre).

## LEE AFFEN – Sound Designer

Lee is a multi-instrumentalist composer, music producer and sound designer from Manchester now based in Sheffield. He has an extensive record in producing high-quality creative content in theatre, dance and film, with years of experience in making productions and installations around the country.

**Theatre credits include:** *Who Are Yer?* (Cardboard Citizens); *Jadek* (Imagine If); *The War Within* (Fallen Angels and Birmingham Royal Ballet); *Far Gone* (Utopia Theatre); *Cotton* (AboutTime Dance Theatre ); *Into Our Skies* (Lucy Starkey Dances); *Othello* (Demi-Paradise Productions); *Hansel and Gretel* (Theatr Clwyd); *The Box* (Hawkdance Theatre); *Outside the Igloo* (The Knotted Project);

*Ladies that Bus* (The Dukes); *Sorry, I Disappeared* (Thick Skin Theatre); and *Anna Hibicus's Song* (Utopia Theatre).

**Other credits include:** BBC Radio 3 and New Voices; *Outskirts* (The Bare Project); *Where Two Rivers Meet* (The British Library film).

Lee has also composed and performed original live scores for silent films *Metropolis, Nosferatu* and *The Passion of Joan of Arc*. Lee is a company member of The Bare Project and an Associate Artist with Imagine If Theatre, Box of Tricks and The Dukes.

## YAMI LÖFVENBURG – Movement Director

Yami Löfvenberg is a multidisciplinary artist and director working at the intersection of movement, theatre and cross-arts. Between making theatre and her own work, Yami mentors, educates and delivers workshops across the UK and internationally, and has collaborated with a multitude of diverse artists, organisations and projects throughout her career. Yami is currently a lecturer on the first ever hip-hop module at Trinity Laban Dance Conservatoire.

**Theatre credits include:** *Rare Earth Mettle and Living Newspaper* (Royal Court Theatre);*Athena* (The Yard Theatre); *Notes on Grief* (Manchester International Festival); *Fuck You Pay Me* (The Bunker); *Breakin' Convention* (Sadler's Wells); *Talawa TYPT* (Hackney Showrooms); *Boat* (Battersea Arts Centre); *Fierce Flow* (Birmingham Hippodrome); *Kind of Woman* (Camden People's Theatre); and *Afroabelhas* (Roundhouse/British Council/Tempo Festival (Brazil).

**Assistant Director/Choreographer theatre credits include:** *Hive City Legacy* (Roundhouse, HOME, Wales Millennium Centre).

Yami is a British Council and Arts Council England recipient, Howard Davies Emerging Directors Grant recipient, One Dance UK DAD Trailblazer Fellow, Marion North recipient and a Talawa Make Artist. She was on the creative choreographic team for the 2012 Olympics Opening Ceremony and is a member of performance collective Hot Brown Honey. She has a collaborative company called Passion & Purpose that focuses on dance management, creative projects and artist progression.

## SIMISOLA MAJEKODUNMI – Lighting Designer

Simisola graduated from RADA with a specialist degree in Lighting Design.

**Theatre credits include:** *The WIZ* (Hope Mill Theatre); *Sessions* (Soho Theatre Upstairs); *Is God Is* (Royal Court Theatre); *J'ouvert* (Theatre503/Harold Pinter Theatre); *Lucid* (New Public Company); *Tiger Under the Skin* (New Public Company); *Driving Miss Daisy* (York Theatre Royal); *Invisible Harmony* (Southbank Centre); *Just Another Day and Night* (The Place) and *Living Newspaper Edition 6* (Royal Court Theatre).

**Associate theatre credits include:** *The Shark Is Broken* (Ambassadors Theatre): *Carousel* (Regent's Park Open Air Theatre); *The Old Bridge* (Bush Theatre); *Shoe Lady* (Royal Court Theatre); *15 Heroines* (Jermyn Street Theatre); and *Herding Cats* (Soho Theatre Downstairs).

## NEETA SARL – Musician/Composer

A wildly innovative and versatile artist, Neeta is an electronic musician, composer, vocalist and producer. A classically trained pianist, Neeta grew up on a diet of Indian classical, Bollywood and RnB before discovering a deep passion for songwriting and electronic music.

**Theatre credits include:** *Love Reign* (Young Vic); *How to Save the Planet When You're a Young Carer and Broke* (Roundhouse).

Neeta's debut solo album *Beat Tape Vol. 1*, released earlier this year, is scattered with unique sounds and synths she created out of everyday objects, like stones, twigs, kettles and air vents.

## TARA USHER – Set and Costume Designer

Tara is a Kent/London-based set and costume designer. She trained at Wimbledon College of Art and now works across musical, dance and drama productions, more recently branching out into short films and teaching at East 15 Acting School throughout the pandemic.

In 2019 her design for *Little Baby Jesus*, collaborating with director Tristan Fynn-Aiduenu, won the JMK Award, spotlighting them as the youngest duo to have been granted the award.

**Theatre credits include:** *The Prince and the Pauper* (Trinity Theatre); *David Copperfield* (Barn Theatre); 2019 JMK Award-winning production of *Little Baby Jesus* (Orange Tree Theatre); *Queen of the Mist* (Charing Cross Theatre); *Heart of Darkness Immersive Experience* (Marlowe Theatre); *A Midsummer Night's Dream* (UK summer tour with Immersion Theatre); *The Barber of Seville* (Surrey Opera tour); *Nuns* (Tristan Bates Theatre); *Sweet Like Chocolate Boy* (Brockley Jack and UK tour); *See Me for Myself* (Tabard Theatre); and *Sweeney Todd* (Minack Theatre).

## STEVEN ATKINSON – Producer

Steven produces in film, television and theatre through Long Acre Arts and Roots.

He works freelance for Theatre Centre and Original Theatre, is a consultant for Theatre & Dance NI and a BFI NETWORK x BAFTA Crew member. He co-founded and led HighTide, producing with theatres including the National Theatre, the Old Vic, Royal Court Theatre and the Young Vic.

## ELIZABETH BOND – Company Stage Manager

Elizabeth is a graduate from Rose Bruford College.

**Training credits include:** *Wondertown* (Ugly Duck); *Blue Stockings* (Rose Theatre, Rose Bruford College) ;and *Spring Awakening* (Stratford Circus).

**Theatre credits include:** *Paperboy* (Lyric Theatre); *Jesus Christ Superstar* (The Old Rep Theatre); *On the Book, Dick Whittington* (Towngate Theatre); *On the Book, Ballet Central Graduate Tour* (various venues); *The Tide* (various venues); *David Copperfield* (Barn Theatre); and *On the Book* and *Beauty and the Beast* (Towngate Theatre).

## MONAY THOMAS – Creative Associate

Monay Thomas is an actor, writer and theatre-maker from south-east London. She is an associate artist at Sounds Like Chaos Theatre Company, a member of the National Youth Theatre and the BFI Film Academy. Monay is currently studying at the London School of Economics and Political Science for a degree in Anthropology and Law.

## THEATRE CENTRE TEAM

Executive Director and CEO **Emma Rees**
Artistic Director **Rob Watt**
Enterprise Manager **Hannah Austin**
Programme and Admin Co-Ordinator **Niamh Parker-Whitehead**

## SHEFFIELD THEATRES TEAM

Chief Executive **Dan Bates**
Artistic Director **Robert Hastie**
Deputy CEO **Bookey Oshin**

### SENIOR MANAGEMENT
Communications Director **Rachel Nutland**
Producer **John Tomlinson**
Associate Artistic Director **Anthony Lau**
Customer Experience Director **Caroline Laurent**
Operations Director **John Bates**
HR Director **Andrea Ballantyne**

### ADMINISTRATION
HR Advisor **Lorna Tomlinson and Lianne Froggatt**
HR Assistant **Neema Gowda**
Assistant to Chief Executive and Artistic Director **Jackie Pass**

### SALES AND CUSTOMER EXPERIENCE
House Manager **Debbie Smith**
Deputy House Manager **Jake Ross**
Deputy Sales Managers **Kate Fisher, Louise Renwick**
Sales and Customer Care Supervisor **Claire Fletcher**
Access and Sales Supervisor **Paul Whitley**
Sales and Groups Supervisor **Ian Caudwell**
Sales Assistants **Sue Cooper, Sally Field, Faye Hardaker, Charlotte Keyworth, Rebecca McQuillan, Irene Stewart, Katy Wainwright, Grace Sansom**

### COMMUNICATIONS
Deputy Communications Manager **Oliver Eastwood**
Media Officer **Carrie Askew**
Communications Officers **Georgina Botham, Naomi Rees**
Multimedia Producer **Lucy Smith-Jones**
Programmer **Helen Dobson**

### EVENTS AND HOSPITALITY
Events and Hospitality Manager **Kelvin Charles**
Deputy Events and Hospitality Manager **Aeddan Lockett**
General Manager Crucible Corner **Anthony Conway**
Head Chef **Natalie Bailey**
Sous Chef **Dan Lockwood**
Casual Chef **John Forrest and Jordan Speight**
Cellar Person **Robin Atkinson**
Events Coordinator **Ellen Mutch**
Hospitality Assistants **Caryl Thomas, Claire Whowell, Cyndi Richardson, Gemma Steel, Grace Parker-Slater, Hannah Lamare, Holly Kempton, James Doolan, James O'Shea, Jessica Goh, Joanne Hall, Jorja Holmes, Judith Flint, Kate Hunter, Kyle**

Baker, Laura Hewitt, Luke Lincoln, Maya Andrews, Megan Peace, Megan Leybourne, Michael Broughton, Olivia Barton, Peter Leigh, Richard Sidebottom, Sandra Holmes, Sarah Moat, Sian Williams, Susan Jones, Zoe Jones, Alison Crossfield, Anthreas Charcharos, Antonia Nadragila, Charles Swift, Ellie Platts, George Webster, Georgia Hatton, Gill Crownshaw, Hallelujah Tedla, James Christian, Niamh McGregor, Regan Mark, Ryan Yates, Sophie Thompson, Steven Chapman, Zoe Kempton, Heather Medus

Casual Deputy FOH Managers **Denise Hobart, Lucy Hockney, Adrian Tolson, Joe White**

Restaurant Staff **Curtis Fairest, Eleanor Johnson, Georgina Beresford, Phelo Bird**
Hospitality Supervisors **Gregory Knowles, Harris Slater**

FOH Assistants **Anne Archer, Hester Astell, Stephen Athey, Belinda Beasley, Marianne Bolton, George Bowley, Lauren Browes, Mari Bullock, Lorna Byrne, Terry Byrne, Julie Cartwright, Jane Challenger, Yolanda Collier, Lilli Connelly, Gillian Crossland, John Daggett, Marie Darling, Rebecca Davison, Sandra Eddison, Connie Fiddament, Kate Flood, Maureen Foster, Harry Foster-Major, Daisy Frossard, Emeline Gilhooley, Jake Goode, Samantha Green, Nick Henry, Rebecca Hill, Merlin Inamdar, Tilly Ireson, Rosie Kat, Bethany Kinross, Alex Lamb, Diane Lilleyman, Margaret Lindley, Christine Monaghan, Sylvia Mortimer, Susan Newman, Elizabeth Owen, Kourtney Owen, Holly Parker, Jodie Passey, Ann Phenix, Heather Reynolds, Isobel Simmonite, Sharon Stone, Daniel Thorpe, Beverley Turner, Christine Wallace.**

Fire Persons **Emma Chapman, Vicky Cooper, Jon Robinson, Lucy Proctor, Susanne Palzer**

**FACILITIES AND TECHNICAL**
Deputy Operations Manager **Julius Wilson Wolfe**
Operations Officer **Rob Chapman**
Maintenance Supervisor **Julian Simpson**
Maintenance Technician **Richard Powell-Pepper**
House Assistants **Josh Allen, Adam Battey, Andrew Battey, David Hayes, James McCready, Kate Wilkinson, Richard Winks**
Head Cleaner **Tracey Kemp**
Deputy Head Cleaner **Pamela Jackson**
Cleaners **Susan Baxter, Louisa Cottingham, Yvonne Dwyer, Gail Fox, Diane Sayles, Diane Turton, Karen Walker, Alan Scott, Carl Phipps, Mark Hall**
Head of Technical Operations **Gary Longfield**
Deputy Head of Lighting **Chris Brown**
Lighting Technicians **Neale Franklin, Kati Hind, Jonathan Payne**
Head of Sound and Video **Nick Greenhill**
Deputy Head of Sound **Chris Ellis**
Deputy Heads of Stage **Dave Pumford, James Turner**
Stage Technicians **Chris Platts, Liam Roughley, Dan Stephens**
Theatre Technician **Andy Sulley, Paulina Chochulska**
Head of Workshop **Nathan King**
Casual Lighting Crew **Phil Baines, Stuart Bown, Nichola Clayton, Peter Conn, Adam Drabble, Jodi Garth, Jack Hyland, Paul Minott, Sophie Slater,**
Casual Stage Crew **Martin Bailey, Benedict Barrow, Frederick Davidson, Shannon Duffy, Alexander Hackett, Jack Hewitt, Robert Lee, Matt Orme, Joe Philpott, Daniel Raddings, Riona Shergold, Mohammed Shezad, Tom Smith, Joshua White, Tom Whittaker**

**FINANCE**
Finance Manager **Christine Drabble**
Finance Officer **Lesley Barkworth-Short**

Payroll and Finance Officer **Jean Deakin**
Finance Assistants **Lindsey Lowe, Lindsey Revill**

### FUNDRAISING
Fundraising Manager **Elizabeth Barran**
Individual Giving Officer **Leah Woffenden**
Partnerships Development Officer **Laura Winson**

### LEARNING
Creative Projects Manager **Emily Hutchinson**
Participation Coordinator **Dawn Richmond-Gordon**
Learning Officers **Georgina Stone, Malika Sykes**
Project Manager **Sally Wilson**
Community Engagement Assistant **Carys Thomas**
Workshop and Project Assistant **Cerowyn Browne, Conal Gallagher, Joe Kinch, Morven Robinson, Noor Sobka, Ruth Lee**

### PRODUCING TEAM
Company Manager **Andrew Wilcox**
New Work Co-ordinator **Ruby Clarke**
Talent Development Co-ordinator **Tommi Bryson**
Agent for Change **Ben Wilson**
Assistant Producer **James Ashfield**
Production Manager **Stephanie Balmforth**
Stage Manager **Sarah Gentle**
Deputy Stage Manager **Sarah Greenwood**
Assistant Stage Manager **Rosalind Chappelle**
Head of Wardrobe **Debbie Gamble**
Deputy Heads of Wardrobe **Abi Nettleship, Merle Richards-Wright**
Wardrobe and Wig Mistress **Valerie Atkinson**
Cutters **Silvia Devilly, Kate Harrison, Imogen Singer**
Wardrobe Assistant **Rose Jennings**
Dressers **Jess Atkinson, Jessica Bull, Sarah Cook, Katherine Gara, Leah Garratty, Abigail Hindley, Zoe Kotonou, Martha Lamb, Eleano**r **McBurnie, Jennifer Moore, Angela Platts, Anouchka Santella, Amanda Thompson**
Audience Trainees **Helen Denning, Jessica Smith, Jess Watson**
Production Trainees **Francis Leeson, Megan Gampell, Rebecca Mayer**

**Theatre Centre and Sheffield Theatres would like to thank the following people:**
Jonas Andrew Philip, Xavion Campbell-Brown, Holly Causer, Titilola Dawudu, Emily Denton, Vincent Ikegbunam, Miles Muwanga-Blizzard, Maria Onafowokan, Alexandra Perricone, Theatre Centre Future Makers, Theatre Peckham, Nerinne Truman, Natalie Wilson.
Zeena Rasheed, drama teacher, and students at Penistone Grammar School.
Ms E. Warren, Co-Head of Drama and Students at Newfield School.
We would like to celebrate Aine Lark, and to mark the huge and joyful contribution she made as Chair of National Drama.

# Human Nurture

**Characters**

**Harry**, *rough around the edges, eighteen, male*

**Runaku (Roger)**, *energetic, fun, seventeen, male*

*We hear the sounds of traffic, people shouting and police sirens.*

**Harry** *is alone in his flat sat pondering, miserable like he has the weight of the world on his shoulders.*

*His phone keeps going off. He eventually looks at the display then puts it back down again.*

*He takes a seat. Then the phone goes off again. This time* **Harry** *picks it up and answers.*

**Harry** Hey, man . . . Yea I know right . . . Yea I'm good, you know me can't get me down . . . Nothing much just a quiet one . . . Yea, thanks, Jono, yea, I mean I weren't looking to do much but –

*Bang bang bang!*

**Harry** *is startled.*

*Bang bang bang!*

**Harry** (*to the door*) Who is it?

**Runaku** (*offstage*) Me

**Harry** Who?

**Runaku** (*offstage*) Me, me

**Harry** Who's me?

**Runaku** (*offstage; comically*) Your sweetest dreams or your worst nightmare!

**Harry** (*to the phone*) One sec, Jono mate, let me call you back . . . yea everything is fine.

*He hangs up the call.*

Look. Go away, you dickhead!

**Runaku** (*offstage*) Open up!

**Harry** I don't want no trouble yea, fuck off or I'm calling the police!

**Runaku** (*offstage*)    You do that and I kidnap Mr Flufflebutt!

**Harry**    I said fu – . . . what?

**Runaku** (*offstage*)    You don't let me in and the Flufflebutt gets it, I ain't playing with you!

*Silence.*

**Harry** *opens the door and* **Runaku** *runs inside at speed almost knocking* **Harry** *off his feet.*

**Harry**    Flufflebert not Flufflebutt, you idiot, why would I call it Flufflebutt.

**Runaku**    Why would you have a dusty little bear that smelt like raw saliva and cheap hair gel?

**Harry**    What are you doing here?

**Runaku**    You used to take that stinky bear with you everywhere, on some weird Mary had a little lamb type shit.

**Harry**    What's wrong with you, why can't you knock doors like a regular human.

**Runaku**    That cheap gel got everywhere. Remember when you used to do that Jedward pineapple look thing? That was mad!

**Harry**    Remember when you tried to do it too? That was mad!

**Runaku**    Yea the ancestors were pissed!

*They both laugh together, taking one another in for the first time tonight.*

*They then begin to do the* Dragon Ball Z Fusion *dance.*

**Both**    Fu-sion Ha!

*They both laugh.* **Runaku** *attempts to hug* **Harry**.

**Harry**    Can you relax please?

**Runaku**   Happy birthday, bro! I told you I would never forget . . . Is it shoes off?

**Harry**   You think I'm gonna let you have your naked toes all over my new flat?

**Runaku** (*laughs*)   I've got socks on, you idiot.

*They both laugh.*

Big one eight! You don't look a day over thirty-five.

**Harry**   Shut up.

**Runaku**   How've you spent it?

**Harry**   Work!

**Runaku**   Seriously?

**Harry**   Not all of us got six A*s at GCSE, we gotta earn our keep.

**Runaku**   Well, you might have if you cared to sit them.

**Harry**   Would they let me?! Said I wasn't turning up to school enough so the geniuses decided to suspend me.

**Runaku** *laughs.*

**Harry**   So you going uni then?

**Runaku**   Yea . . . my first choice is Reading.

**Harry**   Reading?

**Runaku**   Yea . . . what?

**Harry**   Nothing, just far innit?

**Runaku**   Far from what? The whole entire world is our oyster baby!

**Harry**   I'm good here, man.

**Runaku**   Course you are! You know they say misery loves company, but you . . . you seem to be all good on your own.

**Harry**   Why would I be celebrating the fact that eighteen years ago two people that have never even liked each other decided to have sex, and now I've gotta pay rent, bills and a service charge?

**Runaku** (*laughs*)   What's wrong with you, man?

**Harry**   It's a scam! I even refused to come out of the womb and they just pulled me out anyway.

**Runaku**   'Man sues parents for being born without his consent.'

**Harry**   I would! If I only knew where either of those idiots were . . .

**Runaku**   . . . Didn't call then?

**Harry**   My mum sent me a visitor request from God knows where this time, my dad is somewhere playing happy families talking about how he 'definitely will come down and visit'. It's cool, mate, I'm not six years old anymore, don't need any visitors.

**Runaku**   I know, you're eighteen going on eighty-eight.

**Harry**   How'd you even get here, man?

**Runaku**   I DM'd Kirsty, said I wanted to surprise you. She said you'd be at home feeling sorry for yourself . . . And . . . She. Is. Correct!

**Harry**   Why. Are. Her. DM's still open?

**Runaku** *laughs.*

**Runaku**   She coming over? Would love to finally meet her.

**Harry**   We fell out!

**Runaku**   On your b-day? How convenient for her?

*He laughs.*

**Harry**   She thinks the TikTok I put up last night was 'incredibly problematic and highly antagonist'.

**Runaku**   Oh wow /

**Harry**   I know right . . . showing off cos she got a B in her English A levels.

**Runaku**   No I mean /

**Harry**   Been fighting a lot lately, man, she always has something to say about something I've said. She thinks just cos her parents rent a villa in Portugal that she's 'worldly'.

**Runaku**   Ahh, pudding, come and tell aunty.

**Harry**   Shut up, you idiot! Plus. It's a bit sticky for me right now, if you hadn't realised. I have very real people wanting to end my real life over things that happen on the fake internet.

**Runaku**   Look man /

**Harry**   Everyone loves freedom of speech until you really have something to say, right?

**Runaku**   I . . . er . . . I /

**Harry**   You see where I was coming from though, right?! Catch-22 innit – be hated for speaking up, hate yourself for not speaking up. Far as I'm concerned everyone can cry me a river and save on water.

**Runaku**   Pshhh I mean . . . I can't make too much sense out of all that mess you just said but I guess /

**Harry** *looks up at* **Runaku** *ready to hear what he has to say.*
**Runaku** *goes to speak but can't.*

**Runaku**   Maybe it's best that it's just the two of us tonight anyway cos /

**Harry**   You ever blocked someone whilst they're still typing? Top-tier feeling! /

**Runaku**   Look, Harry.

**Harry** *holds his phone up to make a video.*

**Harry**    Just a quick one to say that, if you get caught in the crossfires this week, understand that it's nothing personal – you're probably just an uptight dickhead. And I hate that. Smiley face.

**Runaku**    Harry!

**Harry**    Yea . . . What . . .?

**Runaku**    Look . . . Look . . . Look . . . At us, man, far cry from where we said we would be age eighteen right?

*They share eye contact.*

**Harry** (*laughs*)    Don't say it, man.

**Runaku** (*announcer voice*)    Listen up and up the listening!

**Harry**    Stop, bro!

**Runaku**    MC Tigger, and MC Biggs . . . the UK'S FINEST, the one and only, two and only, colder than frosted flakes.

*A old skool grime beat kicks in.*

**Runaku**
   I'm MC Bigger aka Biggs
   I'm MC Bigger aka Biggs
   I'm MC Bigger aka Biggs.
   I'm big and bad and bad and big
   I'm big and bad and bad and big /

**Harry**
   Try test me I'll snatch your mum's wig
   Try test me I'll eat you like figs.
   Try test me I'll smoke you like cigs.

**Both**
   Cos I can't have a joke and I can't have a laugh.
   Everything said goes straight to my heart
   Try test me I'll throw you like darts.
   Try test me I'll tear you apart.
   Try test me you'll see me get dark!
   See me get dark? See me get dark!

*The boys begin jumping around the flat with excitement.*

**Runaku**   Oiiiiiiiii! (*Sarcastically.*) Brap brap! Blop-blop!

**Harry**   Fire, fire, fire!

**Runaku**   I had one set of bars.

**Harry**   On repeat all day.

**Runaku**   All year.

**Harry**   Proper thought we were gonna be massive, right?

**Runaku**   Huge! One direction huge!

**Harry**   More like no direction.

**Runaku**   That was dead!

**Harry**   MC Biggs, you know, almost forgot how chubby you used to be /

**Runaku**   I wasn't chubby just big boned innit!

**Harry**   So over time your bones just slimmed down then did they?

**Runaku** (*laughs*)   Leave me alone, man.

**Harry**   Ahahahaha! Good times though, right?

**Runaku**   Yea, man.

*The boys laugh and take a moment to reflect.*

**Harry**   You bring drinks?

**Runaku**   I've got the face of a baby cherub, who's serving me alcohol, bro?

**Harry**   It's my eighteenth man!

**Runaku**   Great! Not mine for two months though, yesterday I got ID'd for buying flipping deodorant.

**Harry**   You got cake though right?

**Runaku**   You know this man!

**Harry**    Caterpillar?

**Runaku**    Would I ever let the side down?

**Harry** (*Denzel voice*)    My man!

**Runaku**    You got a knife and saucer or something?

**Harry**    Saucer? Wow is that what that posh college is teaching you then?

**Runaku**    It's not posh it just has a really, really good Ofsted report and it's really hard to get /

**Harry**    Cool story, bro. Yea, wait, hold on, let me travel back to *Downton Abbey* days, and ask the 'squire' if he's got a couple 'saucers' spare.

*He goes to find a knife and saucer.*

**Runaku**    Shut up, what do you call it then?

**Harry**    A little plate! That's what we've always called it.

**Runaku**    Whatever.

**Harry**    Lemme see what the last tenant left behind.

**Runaku**    OK, yea, well, that's definitely nasty.

**Harry**    Journey long?

**Runaku**    Just under two hours.

**Harry**    Shit! Surprised your uncle let you come this far, no curfew today no?

**Runaku**    It's not a curfew, he just wants to know where I am and stuff . . .

**Harry**    It's weird, man. I bet he's doing your head in.

**Runaku**    I mean I think he's convinced that I got a whole Computer Science AS just to help him with his iPhone, and he has a lot more rules then Rita's home, and everyone is . . . I mean we're all Ugandan innit, so there's a whole language and culture I've been trying to learn.

**Harry**    You don't have to you know. You can just be you, don't have to change for no one, just do what I do and get used to showing people your middle finger a lot more.

**Runaku** *laughs.*

**Harry**    And if that don't work, just come back up and live with me.

**Runaku**    Life in the independent unit yea?! AKA the promised land!

**Harry**    The promised land! No supervisors or weird uncles telling me nothing! I'm telling you, the peace you get from living alone is unmatched!

**Runaku**    Yea I bet. It might sound mad, but I actually like being there and don't mind getting back at a decent hour, it makes me feel like someone actually cares, and I'm fascinated by the culture and the food and the music, man. It even feels deeper than that, like a sense of belonging that I've been longing for . . . but yea I don't know, man, it's just hard to articulate . . .

**Harry** *doesn't know how to respond so just nods his head deep in thought. This isn't how he expected* **Runaku** *to respond.*

**Runaku**    You gonna show me around or . . .?

**Harry**    My bad. Toilet. Living space/bedroom. Living space/kitchen.

**Runaku** *laughs.*

**Runaku**    You need to be opening windows and stuff though, smells like sweaty socks, sewage and hot balls in here man!

**Harry**    Do you usually go around to people's houses uninvited then start cussing the shit out of it, or is this a new thing you're trying?

**Runaku**    Look I'm only uninvited because you've failed to invite me.

**Harry** *has found something to put the cake on and to cut it.*
**Runaku** *hands* **Harry** *the cake.*

**Harry**    What you on about, I invited you over for my house warming, said I was having Jono and a few mates over, then didn't hear nothing back for almost a week /

**Runaku** *stops in his tracks. Something has triggered him so he takes a moment to compose himself and change subject.*

**Runaku**    Hashtag team Colin.

**Harry**    What?

**Runaku**    Caterpillar cake, man, stay focused.

**Harry**    We were always team Cuthbert?

**Runaku**    What?

**Harry**    Yea.

**Runaku**    Really?

**Harry**    We couldn't afford no Marks & Sparks Colin cake! Aldi versions all the way, mate! No Coco Pops, just Pops of Coco.

**Runaku**    No Corn Flakes just Flakes of Corn.

**Harry**    No Rice Krispies, just Krispies of Rice.

**Runaku**    Na you're making that one up don't try it.

**Harry**    I swear! We had it once, gave me nose bleeds and stuff.

**Runaku**    Alright now I know you're chatting shit.

*They both laugh together.*

Rita did her thing though, never went without.

**Harry**    Yea . . . well . . . I mean . . . We had the Windows 3.1 in 2015.

**Runaku**    Why do you love to exaggerate? /

**Harry**    Teachers asking why my work is all pixelated.

*They laugh.*

**Runaku**    Or the huge TV from the Nineties with the fat bum /

**Harry**    The TV with the big bunda!

*They laugh.*

Watching *Fox and the Hound*, over and over.

**Runaku**    Only DVD we had.

**Harry**    Some ancient olden days movie, weren't even in three-D!

**Runaku**    Shut up, you loved it!

**Harry**    I 'liked it' . . . Sometimes.

**Runaku**    That would be us every Christmas, when all the others would go to their families, remember?

**Harry**    How could I forget.

**Runaku**    And we would still look out of the window just in case anyone came for us.

**Harry**    Not me, good riddance and all of that!

**Runaku**    . . . Well, I know I did. Just the two of us, and Rita, year after year, man.

**Harry** *looks away and pretends to do something. This is a memory he doesn't want to partake in.*

**Runaku** (*animation voice*)    Cooper, you're my very best friend.

**Harry**    What? I ain't doing this, man.

**Runaku**    Cooper, you're my best friend.

**Harry**    Bro?

**Runaku**    Cooper /

**Harry** (*animation voice*)   And you're mine too, Tod.

**Runaku**   And we'll always be friends forever, won't we?

**Harry**   Yeah, forever!

**Runaku**   Woahhhh, that gave me chills, feel my heart, it's racing man, gonna beat out of my chest! Feel it.

**Harry** *pushes* **Runaku** *away.*

**Harry**   Stop being weird.

*They laugh.*

**Runaku**   None of that stopped us from having the maddest adventures though, remember /

**Harry**   Knock-a-door-run!

**Runaku**   Na, that game was crazy.

**Harry**   Remember Angry Andy!

**Runaku**   Why would you bring up that one time.

**Harry**   Cos it was the best one ever! It was me, you, Sian and Megan. Megan liked you, that's why she came along, but you were going through that 'oww, I'm weird I can't talk to girls' phase.

**Runaku**   Bro, I was like six years old, I still had flipping milk teeth.

**Harry**   Plus it weren't really a phase was it, cos nothing's really changed, ahahaaa!

**Runaku**   Idiot!

**Harry**   The day was hot, like not like normal hot, like hot, hot, my skin is turning red like a lobster whilst you stand there looking confused- type hot.

**Runaku**   I had never seen anything so messy before.

**Harry**   And you've only gone and kicked our ball over Mrs Henry's fence with your big heavy toes. So I suggest knock-a-door-run and Sian's like.

**Runaku** (*as Sian*)   I know a really good street where I can guarantee we'll get a chase!

**Harry**   We get a few where we manage to get them to come to the door, but none of them with a good chase as promised, then I see Angry Andy's house.

**Runaku**   If Andy didn't live there you would've thought it was haunted, front garden looked straight out of *Jumanji* /

**Harry**   And not the Kevin Hart version either, I'm talking that olden-day Nineties version. Then we rock paper scissors, and I lose.

**Runaku**   As per usual.

**Harry**   And Sian says.

**Runaku** (*as Sian*)   If we get a chase remember to turn left on to Malcolm Street, remember turn left on to MALCOLM STREET, and we'll get our breath back.

**Harry**   So I walk straight up, wipe my brow cos I'm sweating buckets, bang bang bang . . . nothing. Sian shouting to /

**Runaku** (*as Sian*)   Do it again!

**Harry**   I do it louder. Everyone's cheering me on. I'm proper feeling the love and I start thumping down this door like a goddamn bailiff on a mission, man, then all I hear is Megan shout.

**Runaku** (*as Megan*)   He's coming, someone is coming. Let's go!

**Harry**   I look up and I don't see shit so I give it one more . . . and voom.

**Runaku**   That door swings open with menace.

**Harry**   I don't even clock eyes with who's behind it before I run.

**Runaku**   And we're off!

**Harry**   And I'm jumping through this garden like I'm The Rock in *Jumanji*, the new one not the old-fashioned one, and you lot are like five yards ahead and I feel as though Andy is literally jumping on my shadow /

**Runaku**   And I'm running like a man possessed, like my life depended on it. I get to the end of the road, shove straight past Megan like, I'M SORRY BUT YOU GOTTA GET THE HELL OUT OF THE WAY.

**Harry**   Oh yea!

**Runaku**   And Angry Andy's coming quick, all I hear is /

**Harry**   'GO, GO, GO' /

**Runaku**   And I take a right . . . Onto Pimlico Road.

**Harry**   Yea! Why'd you do that?

**Runaku**   Was fresh off the boat, didn't go school in Uganda so I hadn't learned my left and right in time for being chased by a homicidal maniac I guess, but yea, next time innit.

**Harry** *smiles.*

**Runaku**   So I look up, stop running and clock that you've all ran the other way. I wanna go back but I didn't see where Andy went – did he go back home? Did he chase after you? So in my head I think 'lemme follow the road round and perhaps I can meet you guys on the other end of Malcolm Street', then it dawns on me that roads don't work like that . . . I'm lost. So I start calling out to Rita, like a lost bird calling home or something. Then like almost out of nowhere . . . I see Angry Andy opening his back garden gate. His corner house lead round to Pimlico Road.

This was the reason Sian told us not to go this route, she was a seasoned knock-a-door-run pro who knew her shit. I run across the road quick without even looking, I didn't care then . . . boom. Andy snatched me almost straight out of the air and holds me up against a random chalk wall and . . .

**Runaku** *takes a moment to compose himself.*

**Harry**   What did he say?

**Runaku**   . . . I don't know. It was like over ten years ago. All I remember is his hand around my throat and me thinking this is it, I'm going out like this, never even getting to experience going to the juniors' playground or reaching year six and getting to sit on the benches rather than those dusty flipping floors. Then /

**Harry**   BOOM, I run in, 'Get off him, get off him now, before I kill you and you won't like that very much'. I managed to grab two electricians from up the road and convince them you were being abducted by burglars.

**Runaku**   I remember /

**Harry**   Worked though! They got him off you, and I stood there shouting the most amount of shit to Andy knowing that he couldn't touch me.

**Runaku**   Rita weren't too pleased when the electricians told her we hadn't been in the front kicking football.

**Harry**   Yea think we got grounded for about a month.

**Runaku**   It was a week, dude, and we got off two days early for good behaviour.

*They laugh and share a moment.*

Look, obviously I came cos I wanted to spend your birthday with you but I also /

**Harry**   Thank you.

**Runaku**   Huh?

**Harry**   Thanks for coming, man, that train journey sounds /

**Runaku**    It's our family tradition I would never miss /

**Harry**    I know but /

**Runaku**    But what?

**Harry**    I don't know /

**Runaku**    You do /

**Harry**    It's just been a mad couple of years' right? You been down South I've stayed up North and the whole world's gone mad /

**Runaku**    Different . . . Yea, man. A lot has changed . . . And I guess that ties into /

**Harry**'s *phone begins to buzz, and* **Harry** *dashes over to answer it. He looks at the screen then declines the call, facing the phone down.*

**Runaku**    All good?

**Harry**    Yea . . . just . . .

**Runaku** *stares at* **Harry** *looking for an answer that* **Harry** *looks reluctant to give. The phone rings again.*

**Harry** *goes to the other side of the room to retrieve his phone.* **Runaku** *is left to ponder.* **Harry** *returns looking worried.*

**Runaku**    You sure everything is /

**Harry**    You slicing this cake up or is Cuthbert just gonna keep flirting with me.

**Runaku**    It's Colin.

**Harry**    My bad . . .

**Runaku**    . . . Cool, well, let me grab the candles real quick

*He goes back into his bag to grab a set of '18' birthday candles.*

**Harry**    Ahhh come on, man, we ain't gotta do all that, let's just eat.

**Runaku**    If we're gonna do things, then we'll do them properly the way Rita would have wanted. God rest her soul /

**Harry**    God rest her soul. OK, cool, but we're not singing 'Happy Birthday'. I gotta put my foot down on that one man.

*He throws a lighter from his pocket over to* **Runaku**, *and* **Runaku** *lights the two candles.*

**Runaku**    Make a wish, brother.

**Harry** *takes a second then closes his eyes . . . He opens them, takes a deep breath, stares at* **Runaku** *and gives him a nod that suggests he's ready for the cake cutting.*

**Harry** *picks up the knife and cuts through the caterpillar cake.*

*They take a moment to bite into the cake.*

**Runaku**    Decent?

**Harry**    Decent!

*They both share a little chuckle.*

**Runaku**    So yea . . . I . . . I wanted to bring something up with you /

**Harry**    Like what?

**Runaku**    Give me a sec, I'm about to say /

**Harry**    You ain't getting married are you? Ha!

**Runaku**    No, I . . . Well . . . yea, kind of, no, but that's not /

**Harry**    What? /

**Runaku** (*really coy*)    Not marriage obviously . . . Just a GF . . . Kinda . . . I suppose but?

**Harry**    WHAT! Who?

**Runaku**    You don't know her /

**Harry**   Is this like the time when you had that imaginary girlfriend back in year seven?

**Runaku**   She wasn't imaginary, she just didn't live in our neighbourhood /

**Harry** (*sarcastically*)   Oh yea, right of course.

**Runaku**   I'm at my cousin's wedding.

**Harry**   Right?

**Runaku**   And this beautiful girl walks in the room and just fills up my whole eyesight!

**Harry**   You talk to her?

**Runaku**   Of course not! I'm not crazy!

**Harry**   Checked her out on Insta then slid into the DM's?

**Runaku**   Obviously! I'm like, 'Hey, I'm sure we've met before but I'm sure I would remember a girl as unique as you'.

**Harry**   'Unique' – so dead!

**Runaku**   So I'm trying my hardest to not be awkward, and she says 'Hey, I remember you' and I reply 'Yes please, good, how are you too'.

**Harry**   Mate, what the actual /

**Runaku**   Long story, long . . .

**Harry**   You've been chasing her down?!

**Runaku**   Excuse me? I don't chase NOBODY . . . I guess I jogged and skipped a little bit . . . But /

**Harry**   Haha! Yes!

**Runaku**   We went on our tenth date last Tuesday!

**Harry**   Time to pass down the mantle of oldest virgin in the village!

**Runaku**   Shut up! I've just been waiting for /

**Harry**   Blonde or brunette?

**Runaku**   I . . . er . . . What?

**Harry**   I don't even need to ask, I know you love blondes, man, you're obsessed.

**Runaku**   OK, obsessed is a little too far.

**Harry**   Is she?

**Runaku**   No

**Harry**   Brunette! Wow! Welcome to the dark side, man!

**Runaku**   Something like that /

**Harry**   What's her name then?

**Runaku**   What?

**Harry**   What's her name!

**Runaku**   Oh /

**Harry**   You forgot? This is the same thing you did with the last imaginary girlfriend! /

**Runaku**   Ohemaa!

**Harry**   What'd you call me?

**Runaku**   Ohemaa . . . That's her name innit . . .

**Harry**   . . . For real?

**Runaku**   Yea   For real.

**Harry**   What . . . I mean where . . . I mean . . .

**Runaku**   She's Gambian.

**Harry**   . . . Like . . . Africa?

**Runaku**   Where's Gambia, bro?

**Harry**   She on a gap year kind of thing?

**Runaku**   She. Is. Gambian!

**Harry**   Fresh?

**Runaku**   As in? . . .

**Harry**   Accent?

**Runaku**   Slight.

**Harry**   Is she like . . .

**Runaku**   What?

**Harry**   Like . . . Like . . . Your colour . . . or . . . Like /

**Runaku**   She's Black, bro! You know it's not illegal to say Black?

**Harry**   MATE!

**Runaku**   WHAT!

**Harry**   I didn't know you were into . . . Black girls!

**Runaku**   Guess I just didn't know any . . .

**Harry**   . . . Damn . . .

**Runaku**   She's beautiful.

**Harry**   Yea . . . I mean, yea, no, of course yea /

**Runaku**   And thoughtful and loving and crazy smart too

**Harry**   Wow . . . er . . . wow . . .

*Awkward silence.*

**Runaku**   But yea . . . I'm telling you, my cousin's wedding was just magical, like some type of carnival or something, never seen anything like it.

**Harry**   Yea?

**Runaku**   Yea, man! Trust me next one I'm bringing you, you'll love it.

**Harry**   Me doing all that dancing with my four left feet yea?

**Runaku**    I'm literally learning the moves myself, it's just a good vibes innit.

**Harry**    Yea . . . maybe.

**Runaku**    What?

**Harry**    . . . It'll be weird . . . I'll be the only White boy.

**Runaku**    Maybe, maybe not, what does that /

**Harry**    Doubt I'll be able to relate to anything.

**Runaku**    What?! I've had to /

**Harry**    You've changed.

**Runaku**    . . . Ha, I don't change I just glow up.

**Harry**    So how long have you guys been together then?

**Runaku**    . . . Not long at all about four or five months now.

**Harry**    Four or five months! That's around the same time I've been with Kirsty.

**Runaku**    Give or take a few weeks.

**Harry**    And you're only telling me now?

**Runaku**    No big deal, we just like to keep things more private.

**Harry**    Why wouldn't you, we've always . . . I always bring up Kirsty . . . I thought we were . . .

*Silence.* **Runaku** *looks away.*

**Runaku**    Look, Harry . . .

**Harry**'s *phone goes off.*

*He jumps up to look for it. The phone is next to* **Runaku.**

**Runaku**    It's cool I got it, bro.

**Harry**    Na it's fine just leave it.

**Runaku** *picks up the phone.*

**Harry**    I said it's fine, man, just leave it!

*Silence.*

**Runaku** *hands the phone over to* **Harry**.

**Harry** *looks at the caller ID, answers the phone and begins stepping away from* **Runaku**.

**Harry** (*all bravado*)    Yea, you alright?

Yea, you see the one I just put up? Mad! work.txt. Yea, just didn't wanna make a fuss, have one every year, right? Haha. Just a chilled one yea, er, yea, just me . . . just me and . . . No, I mean no it's all good you don't have to do that, OK . . . er . . . OK, man . . . later . . .

*He hangs up and puts the phone in his pocket, then turns to a less than unimpressed* **Runaku**.

**Runaku**    Jono?

**Harry**    What ? . . .

**Runaku**    . . . Cool.

**Harry**    Don't do that, Kirsty does that.

**Runaku**    Whatever innit /

**Harry**    And that too . . . Look, he's my mate ain't he?

**Runaku**    Is he? Because last time I was down /

**Harry**    You ain't my only mate you know /

**Runaku**    Bet. I just thought since /

**Harry**    Listen, Roger, man /

**Runaku**    Runaku!

**Harry**    What?

**Runaku**    My name's Runaku.

**Harry**    Are you being serious?

**Runaku**    I told you last year /

**Harry**    I know I just /

**Runaku**    What?

**Harry**    Didn't know you wanted *me* to call you that /

**Runaku**    OK . . . Cool . . . well now you /

**Harry**    Like I actually know you in real life.

**Runaku**    As opposed to /

**Harry**    All your new online 'bredrins'.

**Runaku**    Wow. Strike one! /

*Silence.* **Harry** *thinks.*

**Harry**    Fuck off am I calling you that, man/

**Runaku**    My name is /

**Harry**    Your name's Roger!

**Runaku**    Roger doesn't exist.

**Harry**    He existed the whole time I've known you so what you on about?

**Runaku**    I'm sure there's a little Caucasian boy running around desperate to have that name but /

**Harry**    Now you're just being childish! /

**Runaku**    Roger was a name given to me, Runaku is the name I was born with . . . it fits . . . me . . . it's not difficult to under– /

**Harry**    How is changing /

**Runaku**    Re-claiming.

**Harry**    your name to an African /

**Runaku**    Ugandan /

**Harry**   one gonna change anything? I think you're doing too much!

**Runaku**   Good thing I didn't ask /

**Harry**   You've never even been back to Africa! You're from these parts, man.

You weren't raised by Africans, you were raised by a bloody White woman around White kids, here, in England!

**Runaku**   Am I English then?

**Harry**   Wha' /

**Runaku**   You heard me.

**Harry**   Yea . . . Well, yea . . . 'course you are. You ain't from fucking Wakanda are you /

**Runaku**   Strike two! /

**Harry**   This is real shit, not fantasy, and the truth is /

**Runaku**   OK, great, you're gonna White-splain the truth of my heritage for me, let me cut another slice of cake, this is gonna be good!

**Harry**   Look at the state of you, man . . . You sound like one of them!

**Runaku**   What? . . .

**Harry**   This is to do with this African /

**Runaku**   One of who? /

**Harry**   girl, right?

**Runaku**   I said one of who? /

**Harry**   Look, Rog, or Runko, or whatever the fuck-ever you're calling yourself nowadays, I'm not looking to fall out with you over this, yea? Water under the bridge from me, yea?

*Silence.*

So . . . Erm . . . Jono and the guys are on their way over /

**Runaku**   What? I thought it was just us /

**Harry**   I tried to tell them it's a quiet one tonight but they insisted it's my big one eight ain't it?

**Runaku**   Harry /

**Harry**   Nothing too crazy though, but, err yea, look, you know when they get here . . . Could be more relaxed yea, less of all that 'ancestors, White-splaining' kind of thing. They'll bring a few beers, that'll help.

**Runaku**   I think I should probably /

**Harry**   You'll stay, right? . . . Have a drink . . . It's my b-day, man.

*He fidgets.*

**Runaku** *nods his head 'yes' reluctantly.*

**Runaku**   I'll have a Fanta . . .

**Harry**   I got orange squash, but can shake it?

**Runaku** *half smiles.*

**Runaku**   Then I gotta get going /

**Harry**   You cool with that then yea, Jono and? /

**Runaku**   Like you said it's your birthday.

**Harry**   Yea I know but are you cool?

**Runaku**   Why wouldn't I be, Harry? . . .

*The boys hold eye contact,* **Harry** *looks away.*

**Harry**   Thanks, bro . . . I didn't know cos /

**Runaku**   We don't have to talk about him /

**Harry**   He's a bit misunderstood, but who ain't, right?

**Runaku**    I feel like I understand him, I just don't like what I under – /

**Harry**    And since you moved on /

**Runaku**    Moved away /

**Harry**    He's been there for me a lot.

**Runaku**    Do you even like him?

**Harry**    He understands my frustrations and don't let me feel like an idiot for having them in the first place, I can speak openly with Jono, not feel judged or looked down upon, don't have to watch my tongue or fear that I'll get cancelled for saying something how it is . . . Yet I still feel like . . . I don't know, man, like I still feel a little bit on the outside but /

**Runaku**    But? /

**Harry**    I do get a sense of belonging that I've been longing for . . . but yea I don't know, man, it's just hard to articulate innit?

**Runaku**    Harry /

**Harry**    And I know what you might think about some of the things he's said online about /

**Runaku**    Black people, Brown people, the LGBT community /

**Harry**    But I think people look too much into /

**Runaku**    Where should people be looking then, Harry? /

**Harry**    And I don't agree with everything he says or does, but we do have a lot in common nowadays . . . And anyway I can't be racist, can I? My best mate is Black. Ha ha!

**Runaku**    Strike three!

**Harry**    What? . . .

**Runaku**    I'm out.

**Harry**    What have I said? Are we not mates? Are you not Black?

**Runaku**    Cool, umm, yea you're right, man, I don't know if this was a good idea after all.

**Harry**    I never said that?

**Runaku**    Cake, candles? We're too grown for all this now.

**Harry**    Why are you /

**Runaku**    This is all behind us /

**Harry**    What?

**Runaku**    We've clearly moved on! Dumb idea – sorry, man.

**Harry**    Go on then, go if you're going.

**Runaku**    I'm going.

**Harry**    Ain't like it would be for the first time!

**Runaku**    What?

**Harry**    Go! Leave! That's what everyone does innit? Parents couldn't give a fuck, even Rita couldn't stick around long enough to see me reach eighteen, Kirsty is on her way out ain't she, and now you pissing off back to your posh school in London to live with your Ugandan uncle and your Gambian princess!

*Silence.*

**Runaku** *takes out his phone and plays the TikTok video* **Harry** *put up last night.*

**Harry**    I would really love to understand what you all mean when you speak about all this 'White privilege' bullshit. My best mate R-is4Risky, who 'identifies' as Black, can tell you first-hand the hardship I've been through, but somehow I'm still responsible for the misfortune of others just because I am White. So that I may be 'enlightened' why don't you share with me some examples of all this institutional disadvantage you claim to face with more than a flipping hashtag and some weird memes, but I'll wait . . . cos my timeline is full of loopy-culture vulture, pick-me-boys-and-girls, who are more interested in being heard and gaining followers than talking the truth!

**Runaku**    Knowing me for over ten years and still filming that is wild!

**Harry**    So you don't agree then?

**Runaku**    Nowadays I'm constantly feeling like you're just BlackFriending me, bro, and /

**Harry**    Black /

**Runaku**    Friending me /

**Harry**    Could you repeat that in English?

**Runaku**    White people using Black people as props for some crap that they know other Black people don't support . . . English enough?

**Harry**    OK I just thought that /

**Runaku**    And even if I did disagree, my opinion doesn't undermine how the majority of Black people feel on internet, bro. What were you thinking? This is real life, 'not Wakanda'. I ain't just some 'get-out-of-jail free card' when you say or do something racially insensitive.

**Harry**    Racist?

**Runaku**    I didn't /

**Harry**    You seriously calling me a racist now?

**Runaku**    Are you intentionally missing the point or are you just /

**Harry**    So, if I think, have a question or a fucking opinion I'm racist?

**Runaku**    It depends on what you're thinking, questioning or what this opinion is based upon.

**Harry**    Was my video racist?

**Runaku**    I'm not /

**Harry**    Shouting out my Black best friend in my video is now racist?

**Runaku**    I'm not saying it is racist, per se.

**Harry**    'Per se'? So not regular racist then?

**Runaku**    If you would /

**Harry**    Not premium racist then?

**Runaku**    If you would just listen.

**Harry**    So it wasn't racist?

**Runaku**    I'm saying . . . I'm trying to say /

**Harry**    Because this whole, claiming that every little thing is down to racism is getting really boring now.

**Runaku**    It's just way more complicated than /

**Harry**    Was it or was it not raci – /

**Runaku**    No! Yes . . . no . . . look what I'm /

**Harry**    Exactly! It's all nonsense but people have the time to take out of their day to make me feel like I'm the one that's in the wrong, like I'm missing something. What we need to do is normalise freedom of thought.

**Runaku**    Why is it that everyone who says that always thinks the same thing.

**Harry**    So that's what you're really here for then?

**Runaku**    I came /

**Harry**    For a fight? /

**Runaku**  Because I really wanted you to hear from me and not just someone behind a keyboard about how some of your comments, the things you say and the things you don't say, have been triggering me a lot, man.

**Harry**  . . . You being serious?

**Runaku**  Yes I'm being serious!

**Harry**  How long have you felt like this then?

**Runaku**  I don't know /

**Harry**  You do.

**Runaku**  Eighteen months . . . longer?

**Harry**  What!

**Runaku**  When George Floyd was /

**Harry**  Where are you going with this?/

**Runaku**  When Black people were getting vocal about the fact that we had had enough. It always seemed to bother you when I had something to say, like I wasn't allowed to be one of 'them'. I would replay conversations in my head, second-guessing myself. Was I overreacting? Was I the one in the wrong? Maybe I do need to lighten up. It's been draining, bro. Then after your birthday last year I found myself dreading our meet-ups, and would think of any excuse to cancel. If we did talk, I stuck to chatting about our memories because that seemed to be the only safe place for us. I've been hiding a major part of myself just to make you feel comfortable, and /

**Harry**  This why you didn't come to my housewarming, why you've been on slow replies ALL YEAR? Why you didn't even tell me something like getting a girlfriend? We used to speak about EVERYTHING.

**Runaku**  And now I feel like I can't talk to you about ANYTHING . . .

*Silence.*

After the video you posted last night, I decided I had to do something or say something. But I needed advice. So I opened up to Ohemaa.

**Harry**   Surprise, surprise!

**Runaku**   And she put me on to this Ted Talk about /

**Harry**   Argh for fu –

**Runaku**   Toxic relationships.

**Harry**   'Toxic relationships'?

**Runaku**   And how to confront a friend.

**Harry**   Are you taking the piss?

**Runaku**   Dr Keown says.

**Harry**   Who the hell is Dr Keown /

**Runaku**   'If you're trying to just safeguard your mental health, don't approach that person.' So I'm like cool-cool I don't need to approach you, that suits me, but then two mins later he follows it up with, 'But if you truly love this person then I would say you should have a conversation with them' . . . So last night I /

**Harry**   Look sorry to interrupt you mid-bullshit but . . .

**Runaku**   No! You cut me off every time I have something to say like you would prefer to stay blissfully ignorant rather than have to get up and make a real change.

**Harry**   Maybe I don't wanna fucking change, why must I? You wanna know my birthday wish?

**Runaku**   You know that's bad luck right?

**Harry**   For us to remain brothers, for things to go back to the way they were before.

**Runaku**   And I'm trying to explain how the way were, and the way they are were never safe for me. Your ass is getting left behind and that's why you're so pissed off, no one is 'leaving you', bro, people are just moving on.

**Harry**   So that's it then, you've come to say you're moving on?

**Runaku**   Yes! Unless you are willing to move on with me?

*Silence.* **Harry** *takes some time to gather his thoughts. He's feeling incredibly conflicted.*

**Harry**   You know me, man, If something don't look or sound right I'll call it out. A lot of what you have been saying and doing over the last two years didn't feel real.

**Runaku**   Maybe because you have no idea of my reality.

**Harry**   You're not . . . you're not like /

**Runaku**   What?

**Harry**   I . . . I know you . . . you ain't all . . .

*He moves like a gangster rapper/puts up a Black Power fist.*

**Runaku**   Excuse me?

**Harry**   I get why certain people say certain things and act certain ways but you . . .

**Runaku**   Go on.

**Harry**   You're not really /

**Runaku**   Black?

**Harry**   You're MY mate and I know YOU.

**Runaku** *shakes his head.*

**Harry**   And I wasn't 'BlackFriending you', I tagged you because I genuinely thought you knew where I was coming from cos YOU know ME!

**Runaku**   Harry? /

**Harry**   I'm White yes . . . but I ain't never had no privilege, neither of us have, and I thought you might back me on that? My life is just normal, mate. Normal working-class /

**Runaku**   Ever thought that your 'normal' is a privilege that non-White people don't /

**Harry**   You might wanna choose another word when you are talking about a large group which contains some of the poorest in this/

**Runaku**   What shall we call the advantages one racial group has over others then, Harry? Would 'White non-disadvantaged' take you out of your feelings yea? /

**Harry**   'Privilege' is silver spoons, private schools, trust funds – I came from the kind of poor that people, a lot of your mates, don't want to believe still exists in this country. You ever had to watch your parents decide between petrol or food? At five years old, were you making ramen noodles in a coffee maker with water you fetched from a public bathroom? Age fifteen were you left to fend for yourself in yet another carer's home when your guardian dies and your best mate moves to London? Cos that's the stuff that lets you know that you ain't worth shit to nobody! So when woke-a-sexuals like you try and tell me I have 'White fucking privilege', I will continue to tell them how my white skin hasn't done shit to prevent me from experiencing 'extreme disadvantages'!

*Silence.*

We both turned up at Rita's home on the same day, me neglected and you grieving the loss of both parents, we decided to come together and be by each other's side ever since, we grew up in the same shitty area, same home, same school, same friends for the most part, what disadvantage have you been through that I ain't been through too, man?

*The two boys hold each other's gaze. It's too much for* **Runaku** *and he turns away.* **Harry** *goes to check his phone.*

**Runaku** *starts packing up his bag and begins to make his way to the door, then stops.*

**Runaku**    So we're playing knock-a-door-run, you, me, Sian and Megan outside of Angry Andy's house, you've just knocked the door and Megan shouts out . . .

*Silence.*

*He looks* **Harry** *in the eye.*

**Runaku**    . . . And Megan shouts.

**Harry** (*as Megan*)    He's coming, someone is coming. Let's go!

**Runaku**    You look up and don't see shit so you give it one more huge knock . . . and vooom. That door swings open with menace, you don't even clock eyes with who's behind it before you run.

**Harry**    And we're off!

**Runaku**    And you're jumping through this garden like you're The Rock in *Jumanji*, the new one not the old-fashioned one, and we are all like five yards ahead and I feel as though Andy is literally jumping on your shadow /

**Harry**    And you're running like a man possessed, like your life depended on it. You get to the end of the road, shove straight past Megan like, I'M SORRY BUT YOU GOTTA GET THE HELL OUT OF THE WAY.

**Runaku**    And Andy's coming quick all I hear is /

**Harry**    GO, GO, GO!

**Runaku**    And I take a right . . . Onto Pimlico Road . . . Then almost out of nowhere I see Angry Andy. I run across the road quick, without even looking, I didn't care, then boom, he grabbed me and said, 'Get here, you fucking dirty nigger!'

*Silence.*

**Harry**    What? You never . . . You've never /

**Runaku**   I instantly knew that I had never heard this word before in my life but yet understood that it was specifically for me, for me and not you, or Megan, or Sian, it was for me!

*Silence.*

Whilst at home I ask Rita what . . . what that word meant and she grabs me and says /

**Harry** (*as Rita*)   How did you hear that word, Roger?

**Runaku**   No . . . I . . . I . . . I . . .

**Harry** (*as Rita*)   Roger! Don't lie to me, son, it's OK, OK? . . . How did you hear that word?

**Runaku**   I had never seen Rita this mad, like she was about to blow a fuse or burn down the whole neighbourhood. Before that day I was just a boy. Andy introduced me to what it meant to be a Black boy in this country. And I'm begging, literally begging Rita to not go over to Andy's, begging her not to cause a fuss cos then that would point out how different I really was. I have conditioned myself to forget my Blackness to fit in, as long as no one else calls attention to it I'll be accepted, right? I'll be one of you guys. I'll be just like my brother! . . . If you've never had to hide racial abuse, just to survive, then you might have White privilege, bro.

**Harry**   I don't understand, why didn't you say /

**Runaku**   Because as tonight has proven conversations on race are difficult, Harry, and I just about have the strength to do this now, I sure as hell didn't as a six-year-old.

**Harry**   . . . Look I /

**Runaku**   Earlier tonight you said that you wouldn't be able to come to a Ugandan wedding because you wouldn't be able to 'relate'. My whole life I've had to attend things that 'I can't relate to' but I find a way anyway because that's what learning is, about trying to understand other people's perspectives.

If you've never considered what it must be like to live in a place where there are no images locally, in school or in the media that relate to you, and your lived experience, you might have White privilege, bro.

**Harry**   OK, I . . . I get that . . . but /

**Runaku**   This time last year we're in the back of Jono's car, he's driving like a maniac tryna show off, to who, I don't know, then that other guy.

**Harry**   Shane /

**Runaku**   He's sitting shotgun, and it's already weird, cos we're sixteen and seventeen and both of these dudes were clearly over twenty-five! And the vibe felt weird, like they didn't want me there, like they couldn't stand me and you were fully aware of that so kept saying dumbness like

**Harry**   'You know Roger used to live round here, right proper Clifton boy he is.'

**Runaku**   The atmosphere starts to lighten up a bit when Jono slams on some Kendrick Lamar. And for a moment we're all singing along and we're all 'comfortable' and it feels nice, even though I know it's about to get mad awkward when we hit verse two and Kendrick says the N-word . . . Then . . . Boom . . . The car breaks hard at a zebra crossing. It's all silent, then I see this Somali kid staring straight down the windscreen like friggin Bambi caught in the headlights, we see his parents running into the street after him and Jono shouts out.

**Harry**   'You see . . . this is the type of shit that makes us wanna fucking kill yous' . . .

*Silent.*

**Runaku**   And in 'yous' he meant Black people . . . and when he said 'us' he meant White people . . . you remember that?

**Harry**   Yea . . . I think so but /

**Runaku**   Jono tries to gauge my reaction in the rear-view mirror. I knew it was wrong, yet the weight of his stare sewed my mouth shut and glued my eyes to the window as we drove off, Kendrick off, silence. I felt sick to my stomach, man, as I relived my experience with Angry Andy all over again. I turn to you for some protection or comfort or something, you sit there looking straight into nothing doing everything to look straight away from me, cos if you don't speak then somehow that means you didn't see it and if you didn't see it that means you don't have to denounce it, feel shame, or even take blame. Jono senses the mood and says

**Harry** (*as Jono*)   'You, I didn't mean you Roger, you're a bit different, the kid just pissed me off that's all. I ain't, you know . . . racist.'

**Runaku**   'You're a bit different', I was allowed in as 'an exception', 'BlackFriended'. I knew then that I could never truly belong here no matter how many Kendrick Lamar tracks we played.

**Harry**   . . .

**Runaku**   If you've never been reminded about how grateful you must feel to be in the presence of White people, and not be abused or harassed by them, then you might have White privilege, bro . . . It ain't about what you've gone through, it's about what you haven't had to go through.

*Silence.*

I came over to explain to you that you've hurt me, and I'm not willing to continue to move forward just ignoring this pain.

*He lets out a huge sigh of relief.*

What is it Widow Tweed says in *Fox and the Hound*?

**Harry**   What?

**Runaku**   What is it Widow Tweed says?

*A moment, then . . .*

**Both**    Forever is a long, long time, and time has a way of changing things.

*They share another moment.*

*The phone goes off. It startles both* **Harry** *and* **Runaku.**

**Harry** *looks to the phone, then back to* **Runaku.** *Eventually* **Harry** *picks up the phone.*

**Runaku** *picks up his bag and makes his way towards the door.*

*End of play.*